I0428839

THE CODE WORKBOOK

"THE CONSPIRACY TO CRIMINALIZE THE BLACK MALE"

VISIT WEBSITE: WWW.THECODEMYVIRTUALMENTOR.COM IN ORDER TO SECURE ANSWER KEY

M

CS Inspires Inc.
1837Miramonte Way
Lawrenceville, Ga 30045
Email: CSINSPIRES@AOL.COM

Phone: 1-866-686-5836

CS Inspires© Publishers,
© Copyright 2016 – Cornelius Stafford

All rights reserved.
ISBN-13: 978-1530743056
ISBN-10: 1530743052

THE CODE STUDY GUIDE

DEDICATION

Dedicated To My Son
Cortlyn Jimmel Stafford

Son, all the conversations about manhood, character, and faith, were my attempt to warn and protect you from the looming challenges of growing up a black man in America. It is my prayer that I've lived a life worthy of honor and not demanded discipline, patience and perseverance of you that you never witnessed lived out when watching me. I wish you much success and a bright future limited only by your ability to dream, work smart and endure. I challenge you to unveil the KING in you and never fear the responsibilities associated with becoming the man God has created you to be.

THE BLACK MALE CRISIS IN AMERICA

Before the thirteen colonies were formed by America's Founding Fathers, when slavery was in its infancy, a diabolical plan was hatched to undermine and neutralize the significance of the black male around the world. The conspiracy has been to dehumanize black men by imputing his character, and his potential. Before the Founding Fathers of this nation formed a perfect union, plans were already in motion to disenfranchise the black male relegating him to the lowest social, academic, political, economic cast system rank among all of humanity as his life sentence for being born black.

Black male success is rarely promoted and celebrated in American society! The leading television news seems always to feature African American men caught up in the vicious cycle of crime, the criminal justice system, and poverty. The ability for black men to advance and succeed in America is a phenomenal feat worthy of the accolades, admiration, and modeling by young future leaders. This project is an attempt to provide context to the many experiences faced by black men who from their birth desire to be successful like any other person but lack a roadmap to aid in achieving their desired goals.

The "CODE" narrates the trials and triumphs inherent in the journey of black male's attempts at defying the odds in pursuit of achieving success in America. The "CODE" is a black male manifesto of the experience of living in America. Black men rank among the most vilified, feared, maligned marginalized and misunderstood human beings on the face of the earth. The character and honor once attributed to his leadership now stand in stark contrast to the plight of his offspring many of which are languishing in this nation's prisons or lying in local cemeteries far too young, far too soon. It's a fact, black males, die earlier, are more often unemployed, more likely to live in poverty, more likely incarcerated and die too often and too soon. This fate assigned to generations of black men didn't occur by mere coincidence. Discover the secrets of black male success within author Cornelius Stafford's latest release "The Code." More than million American youth responded they would like to have a mentor in their lives when served by the national organization MENTOR.

There are more than 4 million organizations dedicated to providing mentoring services for young people all around this country. These organizations have the capacity to mentor approximately 4 million youth. That leaves more than 14 million young people who recognize the benefits of being mentored. The "Virtual Mentor" was birthed out the need to reach more needy youth with a structured innovative virtual program which leverages social media and online presence to engage and to inspire African-American males between the ages of 13 to 21 years of age. The service provides positive African American role models interested in aiding young black males to mature into productive and fruitful men.

All mentors have undergone a background check a strict set of guidelines are adhered to in guiding the content and context of all contacts with these young men. The focus of all programming centers around providing these young men with life skills, social, political, academic and economic development training that will empower them to achieve individual success. Particular attention is focused on engaging these young men around a goal of graduating from high school or securing a GED. The programming also focuses on improving their social skills which we believe will reduce the number and frequency of in school discipline and expulsion concerns.   If this sounds like a resource you might be interested in, Text the world 1mentor to 97000 today to get started. You can also log on to the "Virtual Mentor" website for more information at www.thecodemyvirtualmentor.com.

.

This workbook consists of a recap of each of the chapters highlighted in the book "THE CODE" The Conspiracy to Criminalize the Black Male. While it would be redundant to cover the material in its entirety, this study guide/workbook will focus relevant assets that will enable to develop a customized success plan for your life.

The material has been designed to engage and transport the reader on a journey of self-discovery. This material will position readers with strategies employed by successful African-American males who have skillfully been able to navigate the challenges faced by black men in America.

Each chapter opens with a quote relating to the major theme covered in the book THE CODE. A pre-test is administered to evaluate your initial level of comprehension of the material covered in the book.

The remaining content focuses a comprehensive study guide the highlights the most important topics covered in the in the book. Thank you for taking this journey. See you in the winner's circle at the end!

Preface
PASSING THE BATON

For African American males to be successful, they must have a mentor in their lives that will teach them the leadership skills to navigate in a hostile environment. Over the years, the debate has been waged as to if a woman or a man of another ethnicity can successfully mentor an African American male. To both questions, my response is yes. Mentors, no matter the race or gender can and have successfully shared their life experiences in a manner that mentees have gained the benefit from their journey.

The distinction in our program and any program that targets African American males is the fact that only a black man can authentically share the daily experience of navigating life's challenges as a black man!

American justice has no always proven to be just for people of color. This chapter builds on the fundamental core principle, without guidance, instruction and direction our young males will continue to repeat the mistakes of old and die in disproportionate numbers at the hands of law enforcement and other black men.

To reverse the current trends as leaders, it is our obligation to show them they have alternatives. The vision of this program's curriculum is to provide a blueprint of proven success strategies to aid young black men in their journey to manhood.

1. Every man needs a _____ in his life. Life is far too complicated to risk getting it right on your own

2. Leaders pass on the _____ acquired over their lives.

3. Young men need positive male _____ _____ to hold them accountable.

4. We aspire to become who and what we _____.

5. If you are the _____ person in the group you hang out with; find yourself another group.

6. You will become the average of the _____ closest friends in your life. Choose carefully.

7. We as a community have an obligation to teach young males how to _____ in this world

1. **List five leadership traits**

1. _____

2. _____

3. _____

4. _____

5. _____

2. **Define the term Mentor:**

_____

_____

_____

_____

3. The urgency to mentor African American males is being motivated by:

A. *The alarming high school dropout rate*

B. *Desire to curb the incarceration rate of black men*

C. *The alarming number of unarmed black males being murdered by law enforcement*

D. *Black on black crime trends in America*

E. *All of the above*

4. Single Black women head of households' make up 77% of urban homes.

A. *True*

B. *False*

5. More than 51% of urban youth between the ages of 18-24 are unemployed

A. *True*

B. *False*

6. High unemployment and few jobs in urban communities are related to the crime rate

A. *True*

B. *False*

NOTES

Chapter 1

MAKING OF A SLAVE

The underlining message of "THE CODE" is that America has intentionally created an environment that makes it difficult for black men to achieve a respectable level of success.

As we have discussed earlier, our people were imported to America for the purpose of fulfilling whites demand for profits and pleasure. We were not brought to this country out of a benevolent goodwill gesture to improve the standard of living for black people.

The view expressed by the book THE CODE is that there was, and remains a conspiracy to criminalize black males in America and all around the world. At the core, the plot is the intent to destroy the image and character of black men. The prescribed strategy has been to displace the black male from his role and position as a leader in his home and respectability within his community. The goal has been to demonstrate on a global level, his unit standing to hold such positions of influence and honor. This chapter provides a historical reference of how such a scheme was concocted and how this sinister plan was implemented.

1. President Obama's election as the _____ President renewed hope America had resolved its race problem.

2. _____ the black male has always been the goal of the institution of slavery

3. All people and things have a _____ order

4. When the natural order of a God created being is altered it becomes _____.

5. Everything created has a purpose. When the purpose of a thing is unknown or abused, you will receive _____results

6. The slave owner sought to reverse the _____ assigned to black men and women.

7. Plantation owners planned that the unnatural role of future generations would be trained into the children through the _____.

8. Girls would be taught and bred to be strong and _____.

9. Black boys would be bred to be _____ strong and _____weak.

1. **America was founded under white supremacy. White supremacists' believe:**

A. *Whites are a superior race*

B. *All none white station in life is to serve the superior race*

C. *Blacks are an inferior race of people that need controls*

D. *All the above*

2. Many of the policies and practices adopted during slavery were intended to dehumanize black people:

- *True*

- *False*

3. Buck-Busting was a practice of :

A. *Breaking the spirit of strong will black men*

B. *Often involved public whippings*

C. *Included sodomizing black male slaves*

D. *Was designed to destroy the character, pride and resistance of black men*

E. *All of the above*

4. America's conspiracy against black males is:

    A. To destroy the image of black males

    B. Reduce the opportunities for his success

    C. Displace black men as leaders in their homes

    D. All the above

5. Religion was manipulated by slaveholders to control slaves:

    A. *True*

    B. *False*

6. Religion was used to teach the slaves:

    A. *To accept slavery as God's will and order for black people*

    B. *To displease the slave master was the equivalent of a sin against God*

    C. *Good slaves who obeyed orders would be rewarded in heaven after death*

    D. *All religions of the world are inherently good*

    E. *A, B & C*

    F. *A only*

7. The mass incarceration of black males during the Regan era was due to the number of black on black murders that took place in 1994?

A. TRUE

B. FALSE

8. The War on Drugs:

A. Targeted urban neighborhoods

B. Targeted suburban neighborhoods

C. Resulted in an explosion in the incarceration rates of black males

D. A &C

9. What is the Prison Industrial Complex?

_____

_____

_____

_____

_____

_____

NOTES

_____

_____

_____

_____

_____

_____

_____

_____

_____

_____

_____

_____

_____

_____

_____

_____

Chapter 2
THE NEW JIM CROW

The New Jim Crow highlights the resurgence in regressive political, economic and social policies that borrow from the bankrupt practices of racism and white supremacy once openly championed in America. One of the challenges of being born a black male in America is the fact we were thrust into a hostile environment that from day one sought to strip us of all we identified with and that made us whole. The post-traumatic stress realized in the lives of ex-slaves is not a myth. On the surface our physical scares appear to have healed but our emotional scares have never been properly dealt with. The goal of this chapter is to level set the impact slavery has had on our community. I use the term level set because acknowledging that our past effects our future provides us all a frame of reference that allows black people to heal as a result of a newly discovered truth that explains some of the behavior and attitudinal flaws evident in our lives. The comfort in knowing we were not born this way but endured and persevered 286 years of trauma. I truly believe not until we are allowed to openly greave and heal the wounds of our past, we will never truly be able to free ourselves to make the necessary changes to take our lives and community back.

1. Slavery was born from greed for _____, _____ and _____!

2. The Slave trade provided Southern plantation owners with a source of

   free_____.

3. Black males accounted for _____% of the slaves imported to America.

4. Black males were disproportionately enslaved because of their ability to_____ long _____ in the hot sun.

5. The _____ Industrial _____represents The New Jim Crow.

6. Private prisons profit from _____goods produced with cheap prison labor.

7. America warehouses more than _____ million prisoners.

8. America accounts for more than _____% of the world's prison population.

9. More than _____% of America's prison population are African American males.

10. African American men make up only _____% of the U.S. population.

SECTION REVIEW

1. **Southern plantation owners launched the slave trade because:**

    A. White people's hate of Africans

    B. Profit potential for Southern plantation owners

    C. A source of cheap labor

    D. B & C

    E. All

2. List five institutions, present or past that profits from selling goods and services produced with cheap or free labor:

A. _____

B. _____

C. _____

D. _____

E. _____

3. **Black males were disproportionately enslaved because they were capable of working for extended periods of time in extreme weather conditions. What percent of slaves were African men?**

A. 25%

B. 45%

C. 65%

D. 75%

E. 90%

4. **How many inmates are being warehoused in America's prisons?**

   A. 1 million

   B. 1.9 million

   C. 2 million

   D. 2.6 million

5. **America warehouse _____% of the world's prison population.**

A. 23%

B. 33%

C. 43%

D. 53%

6. **America makes up only _____% of the world population. (circle)**

A. 25%

B. 2.%

C. 5%

D. 7%

7. **African American males account for more than _____% of the prison population.(circle)**

A. *6%*

B. 10%

C. 11%

D. 41%

8. **African American males make up what percent of the U.S. population?**

A. 6%

B. 10%

C. 11%

D. 41%

9. Please provide a definition of the following terms:

- *PRISON INDUSTRIAL COMPLEX:*

_____

_____

_____

_____

- CONVICT LEASING:

_____

_____

_____

_____

- CHATTLE SLAVERY

_____

_____

_____

_____

10. Match the following:

(DRAW A LINE FROM THE TITLE TO THE MATCHING DESCRIPTION)

Title		Discription
CONVICT LEASING		Modern day prison for profit
JIM CROW		The explotation of forced cheap labor
CHATTLE SLAVERY		Laws imposed during the Civil Rights Movement
BLACK CODE LAW		Laws imposed during slavery to control slaves
PRIVATIZED PRISONS		Renting prison labor to private companies

NOTES

Chapter 3
DIVIDE AND CONQUER

A key strategy employed to divide and destroy the black community during slavery was to foster a climate of distrust among our people. To achieve this, slaveholders demanded the unwavering loyalty and obedience of slaves while at the same time promoting the genocide of our culture.

Black people have always been thrust into an environment to complete with each other. This philosophy of lack suggests that there are limited opportunities and resources available to blacks so we must fight among ourselves to acquire our fair share. By dividing us along the lines of gender, skin complexation, education, income, and others the slave master's plan have managed to sustain itself for well over 300 years.

Gang violence has destroyed the black community. Senseless murders carried out among and within our ranks as a result of the colors worn, or the zip code in which we live. This chapter not only highlights the problems but offers solutions to bridging the gap of discord in the black community.

1. *Slaves were considered property and were valued at _____ of a man.*

2. *_____ _____, former U.S. President owned more than 150 slaves.*

3. *The term _____ _____ was how slave masters justified their views on slavery.*

4. *This slave trader from the West Indies promoted physiological mind control among the slaves. His name is: _____ _____.*

5. *Slaveholders used psychological warfare to turn the slaves against each other by bringing attention to the _____ that existed between them and make a big deal of them so as to create an environment of rivalry and distrust.*

1. **The first slaves arrived in the colony of James Town Virginia in the year:**

A. 1560

B. 1865

C. 1776

D. None of the above

2. **Institutional Slavery became an essential element of the Southern economy because it involved the exploitation of free labor:**
    A. True

    B. False

3. Following are tactics used to early slave traders to control slaves

A. *Shackles and Chains*

B. *Fear*

C. *Bull Wiping*

D. *Buck Busting*

E. *All the above*

4. It is estimated that _____ slaves were imported to the American colonies.

A. *450,000*

B. *1.9 million*

C. *2 million*

D. *2.6 million*

5. The percent of male slaves imported to America during slavery?

A. 65%

B. 23%

C. 12%

6. Following are differences used to create strife among the slaves:

    A. Skin complexion

    B. Height

    C. Work Assignments

    D. All the above

    E. None of the Above

7. The percent of female slaves imported to America during slavery?

    A. *65%*

    B. *23%*

    C. *12%*

    D. None of the above

8. The percent of children slaves imported to America during slavery?

    A. *65%*

    B. *23%*

    C. *12%*

    D. None of the above

NOTES

Chapter 4

DISMANTLING THE BLACK MALE

Black males rank among the most vilified, feared, maligned, marginalized and misunderstood human beings on the face of the earth. The destruction of the black man's character and the displacement from the role of leadership within the home; church and community have long been the strategy to impede the progress of people of color.

This chapter reveals the detailed strategy employed by slave holders to initiate a gender role reversal within the African American community to in hopes of creating disharmony and greater compliance with the operational task associated with institutional slavery. While the seeds of discord were planted during slavery many of the social practices encouraged have been adopted and practiced in America today.

1. The Willie Lynch letter speaks of changing the _____ order of the gender roles within the African American family.

2. The percent of African American children born to single head of household mothers

   A. 77%

   B. 58%

   C. 30%

   D. 22%

3. The percent of two-parent white head of households.

   A. 77%

   B. 58%

   C. 74%

   D. 22%

4. The percent of African American children born to single head of household mothers

   A. 77%

   B. 58%

   C. 30%

   D. 80%

5. African American mothers often _____ their daughters and _____ their sons during early adolescence.

1. **Plantation owners' believed African slaves needed to be _____ before they were suitable for efficiently producing productive commercial building labor.**

A. Challenged

B. Motivated

C. Broken

D. B & C

2. **The slaveholders determined the key to controlling their slaves was to reduce the influence of strong willed by _____ _____ _____ _____.**

   A. Destroying the black male image
   B. Displacing him as a leader
   C. Damaging his perceived character
   D. None of the above
   E. All of the above

3. **During slavery black women were raped by their white masters rendering the black male**

A. Powerless to protect black women

B. The most powerful figure on the plantation.

C. All the above

THE CODE STUDY GUIDE

4. During slavery, approximately _____ percent of households were headed by two parents on the same plantation.

A. 25%

B. 50%

C. 90%

5. Selling off slaves contributed to breaking up the black family.

   A. True

   B. False

6. Approximately 15-20% of single head of household black females birthed children of their slave master.

A. True

B. False

7. Criminalizing the black male has been a strategy to extract the black male from the home.

A. True

B. False

NOTES

_____

_____

_____

_____

_____

_____

_____

_____

_____

_____

_____

_____

_____

_____

_____

_____

Chapter 5
BLACK CODE LAW IN AMERICA

Knowledge arms those who pose it with the power to defeat our oppressors. Slavery contributed to demoralizing the human spirit of the Africans trapped in this endless nightmare. Specific measures were taken by the Southern plantation owners to impose a level of control over these slaves' lives. Black Code Laws were created by Southern state legislators and policy makers that restricted the liberties of the slaves and were designed to impede the progress some enslaved were able to make by imposing far-reaching laws and rules that only applied to the black slave population. An example of Black Code Law was the fact that slaves could not be taught to read or write. Blacks were not allowed to defend themselves against whites in the courts. Blacks could not own land or business.

Code language is today's politically correct way spout relative of Black Code Laws without prospects for punishment. A direct relative of Black Code Law, Code language is as racist if not more than the impact of Black Code Laws just far more subtle. Republican Presidential candidate Donald Trump's Champaign slogan is, "Let Make America Great Again." He also repeatedly suggests to his primary white blue-collar constituents when suggesting the voters should help him "Take Back Our Country." Both are examples of code language when you consider the two times incumbent President, Barack Obama, is the first African-American President in the history of this country. What is clear, America has not clearly resolved her race problem.

1. _____ _____ _____ were created to impede the progress of black people

2. Black males who fail to graduate are _____% more likely to go to prison

3. Those students reading at grade level by the third grade are four times more likely to graduate high school

4. _____ leasing was a post-slavery movement to supply free labor to privately owned companies

5. Privatization of prison is a _____ billion dollar business

1. **"Black Code Laws that were imposed by local and state legislators in the South to impede the progress of blacks. Provide a list of 7 Black Code Laws:**

    1. _____

    2. _____

    3. _____

    4. _____

    5. _____

    6. _____

    7. _____

2. **Nationally, 47% of African-American males are graduating High school annually**

    A. True

    B. False

3. **Black males who fail to graduate high school are 70% more likely to go to prison.**

    A. True

    B. False

4. **Black males are suspended and expelled from class a three times the rate of white men.**

   A. True

   B. False

5. **Private prisons generate $70 billion in profits annually?**

   A. True

   B. False

6. **Vagrancy Laws were used in forcing former slaves to sign labor contracts to work on the plantation. .**

   A. True

   B. False

7. **Convict leasing allowed private companies to use cheap prison labor for profit.**

   A. True

   B. False

NOTES

Chapter 6

THE TALK

Generations of African American parents and mentors have had to set down and explain the realities of growing up and functions as a person of color living in America.

Discussing the realities of racism in America has never been a favorite conversation for African Americans but one that is vital to the survival of our people.

For generations black parents guardians and mentors of minority youth have shared their insights and strategies for navigating the unpredictable and sometimes jaded racist people they will come in contact with; people who will despise them for nothing other than the color of their skin.

Black males are high-risk targets in American society. African American men need to be exposed to leadership, life skills, and social etiquette training by the age of 13 or they tend to fall prey to the streets and their social environment.

The goal of this chapter on the "TALK" is to reach these young men before life hardens them. This section highlights significant elements of the "Talk" that must repeatedly be reinforced with young black males to avert them becoming entangled with the criminal justice system.

1. The _____ is a part of the rites of passage for African American youth.

2. Black males are at greater risk of losing their lives at the hands of a _____ _____ or another black man

3. Teaching and equipping our youth with strategies to _____ highly emotionally charged encounters is our responsibility as parents, mentors, and surrogate fathers.

4. We must never forget everything that is legal is not _____.

5. Teaching our youth to recognize and navigate the _____ they will face because of the color of their skin increases the odds they will make it home safe each night

6. The community must play a role in _____ our youth.

1. Important elements of the "TALK' include:

A. How to engage a law enforcement officer

B. How to select your friends

C. Interracial dating

D. All the above

2. List the five rules you should follow when engaged by law enforcement:

1. _____

2. _____

3. _____

4. _____

5. _____

3. The average age of African American males when the talk becomes necessary is

    A. *13-15 years of ages*

    B. *9-10 years of age*

    C. *3-6 years of age*

4. The number of American youth who raised their hand and requested a mentor

    A. *1 million*

    B. *7 million*

    C. *12 million*

    D. *17.6 million*

5. **The number of organizations committed to mentoring youth in the U.S.**

A. 4,000

B. 7,000

C. 15,000

6. **The number of youth not being served by organized mentoring programs:**

A. 13 million

B. 14.6 million

C. 17.6 million

7. **List five unarmed black males murdered at the hands of law enforcement**

   A. *6%*

   B. *10%*

   C. *11%*

   D. *41%*

8. **African American males make up what percent of the U.S. population?**

A. *6%*

B. *10%*

C. *11%*

D. *41%*

NOTES

Chapter 7

FATHERLESS COMMUNITIES

More than 26 million children do not wake up in the home of their biological fathers in America. Single African American females head more than 77% of African American homes.

This resurging demand for independence represents a departure from traditional family values within the African-American family. The fracture in and ambiguity in the roles and responsibilities of male and female members of the family unit has led to the demise within the African American Community.

While no one single issue created the current trend with regards to the family dynamics within the African American community, slavery, social welfare, changing values and the war on drugs all have contributed to dismantling the once pillar of strength we enjoyed as a culture. The survival of our community is at stake as we seek a solution to reestablishing a value system that allowed us to endure the ravages of almost 300 years of slavery in America.

1. More than _____% of Caucasians households are headed by two parents a mother and father.

2. More than _____% of Asian families are headed by two parent households.

3. More than _____% of African-American children are born to single black females

4. A child born to a single mom is more likely to be born into poverty?

A. True

B. False

5. Only _____% of two-parent African American families with both parents working live at or beneath the poverty level.

6. The _____ _____complex contributed destroying the African-American community due to send thousands of fathers abandoning the children.

1. **Lyndon B. Johnson enacted The War On Poverty legislation to address the rising number of individuals in America who were living beneath the poverty level.**

   A. True

   B. False

2. **Government subsidies under the social welfare system;**
   A. Paid benefits based on the number of children in the home

   B. Paid a reduced benefit amount if a man lived in the home

   C. Often paid more or equal to minimum wage jobs available in the market

   D. All

3. *African American family values changed from the late 1960's through the mid-1980's in that:*

   A. African American women delayed getting married

   B. *Fewer African American women were getting married*

   C. *There was an increase in unwed black women having babies*

   D. *All of the above*

   E. *None of the above*

4. **The "BOSS" phenomenon among today's feminist rights advocates promotes:**

        A. Equal pay for women

        B. The independence of women

        C. The fact women don't need men to take care of them

        D. Self-empowerment and leadership development for women

        E. All of the above

        F. None of the ab

5. **Today more than _____% of children born to single black females headed household's lives at or beneath the poverty level.**

    A. 25%

    B. 45%

    C. 80%

    D. 75%

    E. 90%

6. The War on Poverty was launched under the Presidency of:

    A. Bill Clinton

    B. Gerald Ford

    C. Lyndon B. Johnson

7. America warehouse _____% of the world's prison population.

A. 23%

B. 33%

C. 43%

D. 53%

8. The War On Drugs resulted in thousands of black men being incarcerated for none violent offenses dismantling the black family

A. True

B. False

9. At the time the War On Drugs was being most aggressively enforced

A.   Police focused on urban neighborhoods

B.   The volume of convictions, not the quantity of drugs confiscated   was the measure of success

C.   Unequal prison sentences were levied against inmates based on color of skin

D.   All the above

E.   None of the above

10.   During 1960 more than _____% of African American homes were headed by men.

A.   6%
B.   51%
C.   11%
D.   41%

NOTES

Chapter 8
TRANSFORMING THE IMAGE OF BLACK MEN

Since the first Africans' set foot on American shores, a concerted effort has been made to dehumanize and destroy the black male's self-worth and character.

Worse yet black men have been conditioned to see other black men as a threat and their worst enemy. This psychological brainwashing has led the black on black murder of hundreds of thousands of black males at the hand of his brother.

This chapter takes an introspective view of the leading contributing factors to this the seemingly inherent racial proclivity to commit genocide on our people. It's time to identify those issues that provoke us to violence and engage viable solutions that will curb the level of violence visited upon urban communities by our citizens of color.

PRE-TEST

1. Slavery _____ African males.

   A. Dehumanized

   B. Rewarded

   C. Abused

2. Plantation owners demanded absolute loyalty from the slaves with the looming reality would be killed if they caused hard to a white person.
   A. True

   B. False

3. The Willie Lynch letter points out that plantation owners should seek to breed distrust among their slaves by:

   A. Pointing out the differences in slaves

   B. By allowing some slaves to own weapons

   C. Allowing some slaves to own their own businesses

4. Slaves were seldom punished for assaulting or disrespecting another slave.
   A. True

   B. False

5. African American males are the only racial group that kills each other at alarming rates.

   A. True

   B. False

1. **Black males kill black males in _____% of murder cases.**

   A. 23%

   B. 80%

   C. 93%

   D. 99%

2. Slave owners saw male slaves as a threat to peaceful stability harmony of the plantation.

A. True

B. False

3. Identify the social conditions that contribute to crime and violence with a community:

    A. Poverty

    B. High unemployment

    C. Easy access to drugs and alcohol

    D. Access to Guns

    E. Stressful living conditions

    F. All of the above

    G. None of the above

4. Which item do you feel least contribute black on black violence among black males

    A. Money Issues

    B. Respect Issues

    C. Women Issues

    D. Issues Surrounding Revenge

    E. All of the above

    F. None of the Above

5. **The jobless rate in urban communities'** _____ **the national averages.**

   A. Double

   B. Triple

   C. Is Equal to

6. **Reason Why black men kill black men at a disproportionate rate**

   A. Segregated living conditions

   B. Easy Access to guns

   C. Low Self Worth

   D. Passive Law enforcement sentencing for black on black crimes

   E. All of the above

7. **Untreated drug addiction and mental health issues disproportionately impact urban communities due to:**

   A. Lack adequate funding to treat victims

   B. The taboo associated with mental health challenges in the black community

   C. Citizens limited access to medical services including mental health professionals

   D. All of the above

8. **Black Lives Matter is a movement with a goal of:**

     A. Promoting a race war between blacks and whites

     B. Demanding reparations for labor exploited during slavery

     C. Bring attention to the value of black human lives

     D. All of the above

     E. None of the above

9. **Circle the top three reason you believe black males kill each other:**
     A. Respect and street credibility
     B. Disputes over money
     C. Disputes over women
     D. Crime motivated by poverty
     E. Proximity to other black men

NOTES

Chapter 9

THE HEART AND SOUL OF A BLACK MAN

What does it mean to be a man? With my book THE CODE interpreting the meaning and significance of the Willie Lynch letters were central to our study. Willie Lynch indirectly defined men as those individuals who influence their families by providing and protecting those within his sphere of care. If you recall the strategy, he employed to dismantle the black male was to displace him from his role as the leader in his home and his community. This is the example men must follow to restore the image we once held in our community. Black males and men of all races flourish when Respected, Recognized and Rewarded.

Another important sign of maturity is when a man will sacrifice himself for those he loves. The difference between boys and men is that immature males are conditioned to see life through a lens that values satisfying selfish wants when men recognize their sacrifice, so the family services are the real determinant of manhood.

Last, when a man comes to the revelation of why he does what he does his life changes forever. When we discover our purpose, we are motived to fulfill the promise of destiny which holds the secret to why we were born.

All these aspects including the social and political etiquette necessary to survive in a hostile environment are the lessons we must teach the next generation of black men in America. One of the goals for writing THE CODE was to do my part in trying to restore the heart and soul of the African American male.

1. Ever African American man needs a _____ in his life to be successful.

2. The real significance of life is the _____ you can provide to others

3. It's important to discover your _____ for living

4. Look to connect with those people who hear your _____.

5. Serve others and life will serve _____

When a boy grows up without a father these young men often go through life without their gifts and talents being affirmed by an influential male role model or person of significance in their lives. Young African American men need direction and discipline to be successful in life. This section provides a solution or a blueprint for restoring the image and character of the African American male.

1. **The first priority of every man is to discover his _____ for living.**

A. Purpose

B. Plan

C. Strategies

D. None of the above

2. **The key to identifying one's purpose is to define your individual "VOICE". The four central elements of one's "VOICE" is to identify one's**

    A. Purpose, Talents, Passion & Area of Advocacy

    B. Talents, Team, Thinking and Words

    C. Compassion, Fear , Love and Trust

    D. None of the Above

    E. All of the above

3. Identify what make you special.

- Identify what you love doing?

- Identify the task you perform repeatedly at or near exceptional levels?

- Identify those issues that interest you most

The key to this exercise is to identify those top of mind activities and activities and interest that hold significant meaning in your life. We are all wired with specific gifts, talent abilities and interest that make us special. Take this time to identify to identify these mile markers in your life.

The following are activities I enjoy doing:

1. _____

2. _____

3. _____

4. _____

5. _____

What talents, gift or abilities have you been recognized for or received rewards for doing with the past

five years.

1._____

2._____

3._____

4. Discover what you're passionate about?

Failure and setbacks are an essential element of any success you will ever achieve in life. In order to preserver in achieving your purpose or any goal you set for yourself you must be passionate

Provide five examples of issues or problems that exist in the world that you are passionate about seeing solved.

1. _____

2. _____

3. _____

4. _____

5. _____

5. Advocacy provides a target for purpose to manifest into change.

If you could solve any problem in the world and were guaranteed success without a limit to the resources and the network necessary to achieve the task, what problem would you solve in the world?

_____

_____

_____

_____

_____

_____

NOTES

ABOUT THE AUTHOR

Cornelius Stafford is a dynamic speaker and author blessed with a unique gift to touch the hearts of the lost, hurting and forgotten of society. His messages will challenge and inspire you to fulfill your potential.   Mr. Stafford was born in East Saint Louis, Illinois, recognized among America's poorest cities. His life stands as a testament to the resilience of the human spirit in overcoming tremendous odds. The death of his parents at an early age, the experiences of growing up in the housing projects of East Saint Louis, and his struggles with identity/self-esteem and his personal health challenges are all a part of his resume. It is from this sorted past that Mr. Stafford credits for having provided him his greatest source of inspiration.

Mr. Stafford's passion is helping individuals and organizations to identify, develop and reach their full potential. As an author and professional speaker, Mr. Stafford enjoys empowering people by providing information and resources that enable them to lead more productive lives. One way that Mr. Stafford makes a difference is by sharing his messages of hope through his professional training company, CS Inspires. Mr. Stafford is the author of The M.I.A. Crisis, a CD project that focuses attention on the alarming number of men missing in action from their homes, churches and communities. He is also the author of "Pathway To Purpose a story of overcoming life's challenges and winning!

Mr. Stafford was the former President of 100 Black Men of DeKalb County, Inc. Mr. Stafford was the 2013 Mentor of the Year for the 100 Black Men of America, Inc., an international community service organization with more than 10,000 members and 114 chapters worldwide. Mr. Stafford also has more than 25 years in corporate America at a Fortune 100 company in a management capacity for automotive transportation conglomerate Chrysler Corporation. Cornelius Stafford is also a member of Alpha Phi Alpha Fraternity. Mr. Stafford's lovely wife of twenty-five years is Mrs. Patricia Stafford. They have one son, Cortlyn Jimmel Stafford. They reside in metro Atlanta, Georgia.

Need A Speaker?

Author and motivational speaker, Mr. Cornelius Stafford is one of the most inspiring and empowering speakers on the circuit. His more than 25-year career as a manager an industry professional at Fortune 100 automotive giant, Chrysler Group, LLC affords him the ability to speak on a broad range of business topics. As an Operations Manager with the likes of Chrysler and State Farm, Mr. Stafford has a vast knowledge of the strategies and techniques that separate the most profitable industry leaders from average and subpar performers. Mr. Stafford expertise is the area of process and personnel management. Looking for someone to help you boost profits, reduce employee turnover and increase customer retention and average gross sales per transaction, Cornelius Stafford is your guy.

  As a community activist, Mr. Stafford has assembled an impressive resume of accomplishments. Mr. Stafford is a former distinguished winner of the 100 Black Men of America's Mentor of The Year Award, where he was selected from its more than ten thousand members and 114 chapters worldwide! Mr. Stafford also formally served as the President and Chief Operating Officer of the 100 Black Men of DeKalb County chapter. Contact Mr. Stafford's through his website at:www.thecodemyvirtualmentor.com

Office phone at **1-866-686-5836** *or email at; csinspires@aol.com*

Speaking Topics Include, But Are Not Limited To The Following Subjects:

- *The Power In Servant Leadership*

- *How To Transform Your Career*

- *Discovering Your Purpose*

- *Overcoming Challenging Times*

- *Developing Inspired Employees*

- *Do you Understand Your Value*

- *Mentoring African American Boys*

- *How To Increase Customer Retention*

Consider booking Mr. Stafford for your next event.

Cornelius Stafford CS Inspires Inc.

1-866-686-5836

wwwthecodemyvirtualmentor.com

THE M.I.A. CRISIS

A PROGRAM DEDICATED TO MEN MENTORING MEN

ONE MAN'S JOURNEY IN TRANSFORMING LIFE'S CHALLENGES TO LIFE'S TRIUMPHS

THE CODE STUDY GUIDE

Final Notes and Reference

Related links:

- *Wikiquote,:https://en.wikiquote.org/wiki/Sun_Tzu*

- *legal-dictionary.thefreedictionary.com/vagrancy*

- *Historical Document: The 1865 Mississippi Black Code (GMU.edu)*

- *Life in the South After the Civil War - Study.com*

- *Study.com/academy/lesson/life-in-the-south-after-the-civil-war.html*

- *Here are 6 Companies That Get Rich off Prisoners - Attnwww.attn.com/stories/941/who-profits-from-Prisoners*

- *Economic Impacts of Prison Growth - Federation of https://www.fas.org/sgp/crs/R41177Federation of American Scientists*

- *Racial and Ethnic Disparities in the US Criminal Justice*

- *Vagrancy legal definition of vagrancy - Legal Dictionary legal-dictionary.thefreedictionary.com/vagrancy*

- *Convict lease - Wikipedia, the free encyclopedia https://en.wikipedia.org/wiki/Convict_lease Wikipedia*

- *Black Lives Matter - The Schott 50 State Report on Public www.blackboysreport.org/2015-black-boys-report.pdf*

- *Civil Rights Act of 1964 - Wikipedia, the free encyclopedia https://en.wikipedia.org/wiki/Civil_Rights_Act_of_1964 Wikipedia*

- *America's War on Drugs Drives High Incarceration Rates content.time.com/time/magazine/article/0,9171,2109777,00.html*

- *Black Men Who Dropped Out of High School Have Very www.amren.com/.../black-men-who-dropped-out American Renaissance*

- *Finding Resources to Support Mentoring Programs and* *www.mentoring.org/old-downloads/mentoring_1154.pdf*

- *Stop-and-Frisk Data | New York Civil Liberties Union* *www.nyclu.org/.../**stop-and-frisk-data***

- *Elitism Facts, information, pictures | Encyclopedia.com* *www.encyc*

- *White supremacy - Wikipedia, the freehttps://en.wikipedia.org/wiki/White_supremacy*

- *Cognitive dissonance - Wikipedia, the free encyclopedia*

- *Turf war - Wikipedia, the free encyclopedia*
  *https://en.wikipedia.org/wiki/**Turf_war**Wikipedi*

- *Urban Dictionary: crabs-in-a-barrel* *www.urbandictionary.com/define.php?...crabs-in...barr* **Urban Dictionary**

ACKNOWLEDGMENTS

I thank God for introducing me to the love of my life. I am so fortunate to have you to love. You give me purpose. I love you for life, my wife, Patricia Stafford.

Cortlyn, all I have ever wanted was the very best for you. Keep pursuing your dream. I am so proud to be your dad.

I am eternally grateful for the sacrifices made by my late parents, Jimmie and Donnie Stafford. I strive every day to live a life that would honor and make you both proud.

Jeanette Gregory, my big sister, thanks for loving me for who I am. Your encouraging words mean the world to me.

To my cousin, the late James Williams, thank you for mentoring me through one of the most volatile periods of my life. You saw the best in me during the worst of times. I love and miss you Cuz!

Pastor John P. Kee, you will never know the influence you have had on my life!

NOTES

NOTES

www.ingramcontent.com/pod-product-compliance
Lightning Source LLC
Chambersburg PA
CBHW081410280526
45788CB00009B/3044